W9-BVI-215

WHAT WOULD IT TAKE TO MAKE A

JET PACK?

BY ANITA NAHTA AMIN

CAPSTONE PRESS
a capstone imprint

Capstone Captivate is published by Capstone Press, an imprint of Capstone.
1710 Roe Crest Drive
North Mankato, Minnesota 56003
www.capstonepub.com

Library of Congress Cataloging-in-Publication Data is available on the Library of Congress website.
ISBN: 978-1-5435-9118-7 (library hardcover)
ISBN: 978-1-4966-6598-0 (paperback)
ISBN: 978-1-5435-9126-2 (eBook PDF)

Summary: Describes how the science-fiction concept of jet packs could develop in real life, including the scientific concepts involved, the progress that scientists have made, and what the future could hold.

Image Credits
Alamy: Graham Hughes, 26, MF1 collection, 13; AP Images: Hoch Zwei/picture-alliance/dpa, cover (man); iStockphoto: AmandaLewis, 5; NASA: JSC, 6; Newscom: CB2/ZOB/WENN.com, 22, Ian Vogler/Mirrorpix, 14, Leonhard Foeger/Reuters, 21, Mike Stocker/Orlando Sentinel/MCT, 17; Shutterstock Images: AboutLife, 29, Andrey862, 10, BasPhoto, 25, 28, ChameleonsEye, 18, 19, Kamenetskiy Konstantin, cover (background), Mascha Tace, 9
Design Elements: Shutterstock Images

Editorial Credits
Editor: Arnold Ringstad; Designer: Laura Graphenteen

All internet sites appearing in back matter were available and accurate when this book was sent to press.

Printed in the United States of America.
PA99

TABLE OF CONTENTS

WORDS IN BOLD ARE IN THE GLOSSARY.

CHAPTER ONE

FLYING WITH A BACKPACK

Someday you might strap on a new kind of backpack. But this backpack won't have books in it. When you turn it on, this backpack will rumble and shake. Smoke will shoot out the bottom. Then you'll blast off! You'll zoom into the sky with your jet pack.

Jet packs are in movies and books. The military has tested them. Some people fly them at special events. But jet packs are not widely available. Scientists are working to change this. The dream of soaring like a bird may soon come true.

A trained pilot tests a jet pack.

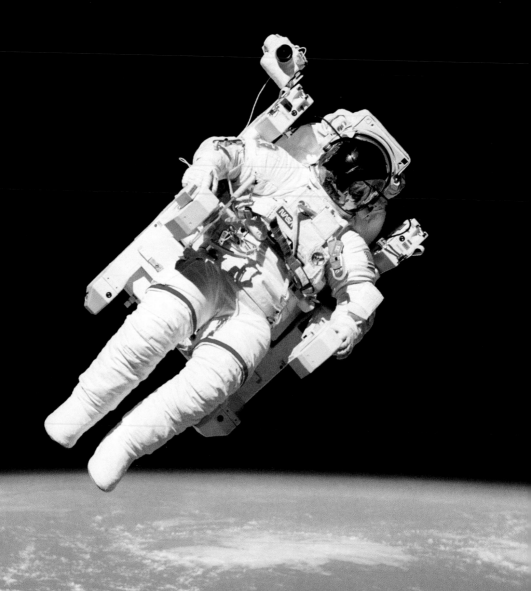

An astronaut uses a jet pack to
fly through space.

CHAPTER TWO

WHAT IS A JET PACK?

A jet pack is a flying machine. You strap it to your back like a backpack. It pushes you up into the air. It lets you fly from place to place.

To fly, a jet pack must work against **gravity**. Gravity is a force that pulls objects down to the center of Earth. Jet packs push upward against gravity. To do this, the jet pack can use an **engine**. The engine shoots out hot gases. These gases make **thrust**. Thrust pushes in the opposite direction of the gases. It sends the jet pack upward or forward.

A jet pack must be small and light. It has to fit on a person's back. But it must be powerful. It has to lift the user. It must also lift its own weight.

The jet pack must keep the user safe. It carries the user high in the air. Falling is dangerous. The jet pack needs to always work correctly.

A JET PACK IN SPACE

Astronauts have tested a jet pack in space. Bruce McCandless first flew it in 1984. He wore a large backpack over his space suit. It shot out puffs of gas. This made thrust to push him around. In space, gravity did not pull him downward. This made flying a jet pack in space easier than on Earth.

HOW A JET PACK FLIES

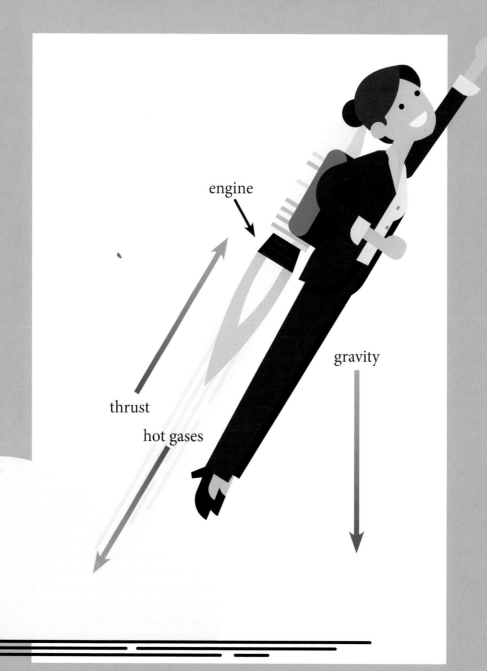

Some jet packs create thrust with jets of water.

CHAPTER THREE

HOW WOULD A JET PACK WORK?

There are a few ways jet packs might fly. One way uses engines. The engines make thrust by shooting out hot gases. Users have hand controls. They can change which way the engines point. This lets them steer. They can change how fast the engines shoot out gases. This lets them rise or fall.

Other jet packs use water. A long hose connects the jet pack to a machine floating in the water. The machine sucks in water and sends it to the jet pack. The water shoots out of the jet pack. This makes thrust. The thrust sends the jet pack into the air. Hand controls let the users change the direction the water shoots out. This lets them steer.

All jet packs need power to work. Engines use **fuel** for power. Fuel is a chemical that burns to release energy. The engine burns the fuel. The fuel mixes with air. This creates the hot gases. Fuel is stored in a tank on the jet pack.

Jet packs that use water can only be used over water. It takes a lot of water to send a jet pack into the air. There is not enough room in the jet pack to hold a water tank. It needs to get its water from a lake or ocean below.

FUN FACT

Jet airplanes have room for huge fuel tanks. They can fly for many hours. Jet packs have much less room. Most can fly for just a few minutes.

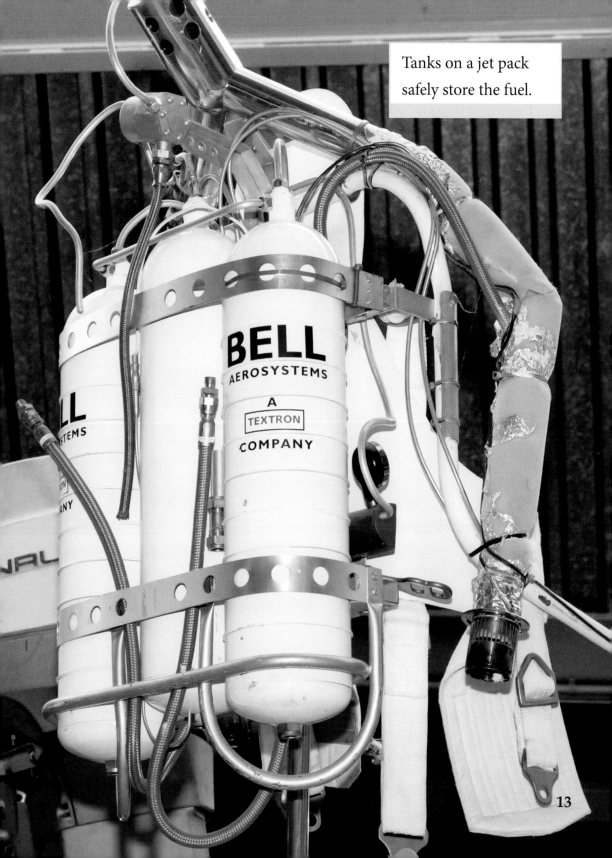

Tanks on a jet pack safely store the fuel.

David Mayman is the inventor of the JB10.

CHAPTER FOUR

CURRENT TECH

There are a few jet packs that people can use today. One is the JB10. It uses two jet engines to fly. Users hold their arms straight ahead. They use hand controls. The left hand controls how much thrust the engines make. The right hand controls which direction the thrust pushes. The JB10 holds enough fuel to fly for about eight minutes.

A newer version is called the JB11. It has six small engines instead of two big ones. It can carry more weight than the JB10. It can also fly longer. It can fly for 10 minutes before it needs more fuel. The JB11 has another new feature. A computer helps control the way the engines point. It makes tiny adjustments to help the user stay balanced.

FUN FACT
The JB10 costs about $300,000.

Another current model is the Apollo JetPack. It carries about 5 gallons (19 liters) of fuel. It turns this fuel into hot gas. Then it shoots the gas out of the engines. This pushes the jet pack into the air.

Flying the Apollo JetPack is hard. It takes many hours of practice. People cannot buy it. People are trained to fly the jet pack before using it at special events. The flight time is short. It has enough fuel for just 30 seconds of flying.

THE BELL ROCKET BELT

The Apollo JetPack works like an early jet pack called the Bell Rocket Belt. A person first flew the Bell Rocket Belt in 1961. The flight lasted just a few seconds. But it was important. It helped inventors think of new ideas for jet packs.

Handheld controllers let people fly the Apollo JetPack.

People can zoom along at high speeds with the JetLev-Flyer.

The JetLev-Flyer is easier to learn to fly than other jet packs.

The JetLev-Flyer uses water. It is safer to fly than other jet packs. The user is always flying over water. Falling into water is less harmful than falling onto land. The company says training can take just a few minutes.

CHAPTER FIVE

WHAT TECH IS NEEDED?

Some jet packs are flying today. But they are not common. Builders must overcome a few challenges before jet packs become more popular.

One big challenge is energy. There is little room to store energy on a jet pack. Fuel is used up quickly. New engine tech might help. New engines could use fuel more slowly. This could let people fly longer.

Weight is a related challenge. Jet packs are made from tough materials. This is important for safety. But these materials can be heavy. Lifting a heavy jet pack takes more energy. Making jet packs lighter could help. They would need to lift less weight. They could fly faster and farther.

Many of today's jet packs
are bulky and heavy.

The Martin Jetpack used propellers to fly.

Another challenge is cost. Jet packs are very expensive. Few people can afford them. How can jet packs be made cheaper?

Some people are looking to **drones** for ideas. Drones are popular flying machines. They are usually smaller than jet packs.

Drones use propellers to fly. Propellers are like spinning fans. They blow air downward. This pushes the drone up. Scientists have a lot of experience with drones. They can make drones that stay steady in the air. And they can build drones fairly cheaply. Maybe some of these ideas could work for jet packs.

One kind of jet pack has already used propellers to fly. It was called the Martin Jetpack. It was a large machine with two big propellers. It could fly for more than 30 minutes.

FUN FACT

The company behind the Martin Jetpack shut down in 2019. But its technology could live on in future jet packs.

Jet pack safety is another big challenge. Jet packs that make hot gases can cause burns. Users must wear special clothing. These clothes keep them safe. They also must be careful near other people when flying close to the ground. Hot gases could harm nearby people too.

Flying high can be dangerous. What if the jet pack runs out of fuel? Or what if the engine stops working in midair? Even falling from just a few feet can be risky. Designers are working on special **parachutes**. The parachutes will fit into the jet pack. They will slow the user's fall.

Steering and control can be tricky. The user needs a lot of training for some jet packs. Computers can help. They can keep track of the jet pack's balance. They can make little changes to keep the user steady. Staying steady in the air keeps the user safe and comfortable.

One kind of jet pack has jet engines that attach to the user's arms. The user can point them to steer.

Jet packs could have many uses people have not yet imagined.

CHAPTER SIX

WHAT COULD THE FUTURE LOOK LIKE?

People use jet packs today. People put on shows with jet packs. People fly water jet packs for fun. But no one uses jet packs for everyday travel. Maybe that will change in the future.

How could jet packs be useful in the future? Maybe people will fly them to work or school. Maybe people will race or play games in the sky. Rescuers could use them to save people from burning buildings. Soldiers could zoom across a battlefield.

Today's jet packs are bulky. Future ones may be easier to wear.

Scientists have worked on jet packs for many years. These flying machines are getting better all the time. Future jet packs will be lighter and stronger. They will let us fly higher and faster. They will be cheaper and safer. You may able to buy one in stores someday. Would you fly one? Where would you fly?

Many people dream of using jet packs. Scientists are working to make them available to more people.

GLOSSARY

drone (DROHN)—a flying machine that does not have a pilot and is controlled from the ground

engine (EN-gin)—a device that burns fuel and releases hot gases that create thrust

fuel (FYOOL)—a material burned to give off energy

gravity (GRAV-uh-tee)—a force that pulls objects together; gravity pulls objects down toward the center of Earth

parachute (PAIR-uh-shoot)—a large piece of fabric that slows down a falling object

thrust (THRUST)—the force made by a jet or rocket engine that pushes an object along

READ MORE

Enz, Tammy. *The Science Behind Superman's Flight*. North Mankato, MN: Capstone Press, 2017.

Salzman, Mary Elizabeth. *Biggest, Baddest Book of Flight*. Minneapolis, MN: Abdo Publishing, 2015.

Sohn, Emily. *A Crash Course in Forces and Motion with Max Axiom, Super Scientist*. North Mankato, MN: Capstone Press, 2019.

INTERNET SITES

NASA: Dynamics of Flight
https://www.grc.nasa.gov/www/k-12/UEET/StudentSite/dynamicsofflight.html

Smithsonian Channel: The Strange History of the Jet Pack, and Where It's Heading
https://www.smithsonianchannel.com/videos/the-strange-history-of-the-jet-pack-and-where-its-heading/36943

Smithsonian National Air and Space Museum: How Things Fly
http://howthingsfly.si.edu/

INDEX